Indira Gandhi

Trevor Fishlock

Illustrated by
Karen Heywood

Hamish Hamilton
London

Titles in the Profiles *series*

Muhammad Ali	0-241-10600-1	John Lennon	0-241-11561-2
Chris Bonington	0-241-11044-0	Martin Luther King	0-241-10931-0
Ian Botham	0-241-11031-9	Nelson Mandela	0-241-11913-8
Geoffrey Boycott	0-241-10712-1	Bob Marley	0-241-11476-4
Edith Cavell	0-241-11479-9	Paul McCartney	0-241-10930-2
Charlie Chaplin	0-241-10479-3	Montgomery of Alamein	0-241-11562-0
Winston Churchill	0-241-10482-3	Lord Mountbatten	0-241-10593-5
Sebastian Coe	0-241-10848-9	Florence Nightingale	0-241-11477-2
Marie Curie	0-241-11741-0	Rudolf Nureyev	0-241-10849-7
Roald Dahl	0-241-11043-2	Emmeline Pankhurst	0-241-11478-0
Thomas Edison	0-241-10713-X	Pope John Paul II	0-241-10711-3
Queen Elizabeth II	0-241-10850-0	Anna Pavlova	0-241-10481-5
The Queen Mother	0-241-11030-0	Prince Philip	0-241-11167-6
Alexander Fleming	0-241-11203-6	Lucinda Prior-Palmer	0-241-10710-5
Anne Frank	0-241-11294-X	Barry Sheene	0-241-10851-9
Indira Gandhi	0-241-11772-0	Mother Teresa	0-241-10933-7
Gandhi	0-241-11166-8	Margaret Thatcher	0-241-10596-X
Basil Hume	0-241-11204-4	Daley Thompson	0-241-10932-9
Kevin Keegan	0-241-10594-3	Queen Victoria	0-241-10480-7
Helen Keller	0-241-11295-8	The Princess of Wales	0-241-11740-2

First published 1986 by
Hamish Hamilton Children's Books
Garden House, 27 Wrights Lane, London W8 5TZ
. © 1986 text by Trevor Fishlock
© 1986 illustrations by Karen Heywood
British Library Cataloguing in Publication Data
Fishlock, Trevor
Indira Gandhi. (Profiles)
1. Gandhi, Indira—Juvenile literature
2. Prime ministers—India—Biography
I. Title   II. Series
954,04'0924   DS481.G23
ISBN 0-241-11772-0
Typeset by Pioneer
Printed in Great Britain at the
University Press, Cambridge

Contents

Indira Gandhi, Prime Minister of India

1   A Woman Of Courage

A great jostling crowd gathered at the funeral ground on the banks of the River Jumna in the Indian capital city of Delhi. The people were there in tens of thousands, rich and humble alike, to say farewell to their extraordinary leader, Indira Gandhi.

In keeping with Hindu tradition her body lay upon a pyre of fragrant sandalwood logs, strewn with bright flowers. Her son, Rajiv, clad all in white, applied a flame. As the fire burned, buglers sounded a salute. Indira Gandhi's family, and her friends and followers, walked slowly around the pyre, casting incense and petals into the flames. Prime ministers and presidents and other national leaders from many parts of the world were in the crowd, paying their final tribute.

After the cremation there was one more ritual. The ashes were collected in brass and copper urns and taken all over the vast land of India. They were sprinkled into rivers and lakes, and scattered from an aircraft over the Himalayan mountains in the north.

Thus Indira Gandhi's mortal remains were returned to the land she loved. She had led the country for sixteen years, and all her life she was close to the centre of important events. From her earliest years her experience was of turbulence, drama and controversy. Her life was part of the story of modern India. She dominated a great country.

She died violently, killed by two of her bodyguards as she walked in the morning sunshine, in her usual brisk and bustling fashion, through the lovely gardens of her home in Delhi. She was sixty-six years old.

The day before she was murdered she addressed a huge crowd at a rally and declared, 'I am not afraid . . . if I die today every drop of my blood will invigorate the nation.'

She had spoken these words many times before. No-one ever doubted the courage of the remarkable woman who had sometimes been called 'the Empress of India'. And no-one doubted that with her death a chapter of Indian history ended.

2 A Famous Name

She was born on 19 November 1917 in her grandfather's house in Allahabad in northern India, and given the names of Indira Priyadarshini. The second name means 'beautiful to behold'. The Nehru family into which she was born was to become the most famous in the land. First her father, then she, and then her elder son, were prime ministers, leaders of the world's second-largest nation after China.

Her ancestors had originally come from Kashmir, the rugged, lovely and fertile region in the far north. They were Brahmins, meaning people of the highest caste.

There are millions of Muslims and Christians in India, and followers of other faiths too; but most of the people, more than four-fifths, are Hindus. Hindus believe in reincarnation — that they will be born again into another life — and they worship a number of gods. Hindu society is divided into many hundreds of castes, or clans, a system that has existed since ancient times. Many castes are based on trades and occupations, and many have their own strict rules and rituals. For example, many young men and women do not marry outside their own caste. The caste system is part of the very framework of Indian life. It is a complicated social scale, with high castes and low castes.

Indira's grandfather was Motilal Nehru, a successful and distinguished lawyer. He was a handsome and flamboyant man, with a ready laugh. He had a magnetic personality and was a natural leader. His son, Jawaharlal, was born in 1889. Like other wealthy men in India, Motilal sent his son to be educated in England. The boy went first to Harrow public school, one of the famous schools of England, and then to Cambridge University. He qualified as a barrister in London and returned to India.

In 1916 he married a pretty and delicate girl named Kamala Kaul. In accordance with Hindu custom it was a marriage arranged by the parents. Indira was the only child.

The Nehru clan lived in a splendid and large house in Allahabad called 'Anand Bhavan', meaning 'the abode of peace'. In fact it was hardly ever peaceful. It was a place of great political activity and of much debate. There was a constant stream of visitors. The house was a centre of the young political movement that was beginning the struggle for the independence of India.

India at that time was an important part of the British Empire. Indeed, it was known as the jewel in the crown of the Empire. The British first went to India as merchant venturers — traders — in the seventeenth century. Gradually, through conquest and the spread of their administration, and with the co-operation of numerous Indian princes and other local rulers, they

Indira with Kamala, her mother

brought a large part of the Indian subcontinent under British rule.

Eventually the country was governed by a British viceroy, a powerful figure ruling a sixth of the people of the world on behalf of the monarch in Britain.

The British brought to India their system of administration and law, a railway network and military methods. They also, incidentally, brought cricket, which became India's national game — and they imported and established the English language. Thus many Indians were exposed to English literature and to British political thought, to the ideas of democracy and elected government.

It was true that, as colonial rulers, the British did not put these democratic ideas into practice in India. But many Indians naturally absorbed them. Among these people was planted the seed of the idea that India should one day be independent and self-governing.

The seed was nourished by the Indian National Congress, a movement founded in 1885. In time the Congress became the greatest political force in India, the heart of the freedom struggle and the main political party in the years after independence.

Jawaharlal Nehru and Mohandas Karamchand Gandhi emerged as the greatest leaders of the Congress and the Independence movement. Gandhi, like Nehru, had qualified as a barrister in England. He developed his creed that the freedom movement should be non-violent. This creed was known as satyagraha, meaning 'truth force'. He believed that the British could be persuaded to leave India and allow the people to

14

govern themselves, as a matter of justice. By insisting that there should be a relentless moral pressure, and not violence, Gandhi proposed something new and startling in a world used to bloody revolutions.

In time Indians in their millions came to revere Gandhi. He was small in stature, humble in his habits and simple in his dress. Usually he wore just a loincloth, known as a dhoti, and a shawl. But his personality was large, and he had the gift of touching the hearts of the people and uniting them in a single cause. He was an inspiring speaker. India had never known such a leader. His saintly qualities earned him the title of Mahatma, meaning 'great soul'. In 1916, the year before Indira Nehru's birth, he returned to India from South Africa, where he had lived for many years and had led struggles on behalf of ordinary people.

In April 1919 there occurred an event of great significance. A crowd of people defied the British regulations and gathered for a meeting in a walled garden in the city of Amritsar, in the northern state of Punjab. General Reginald Dyer decided to teach them a harsh lesson, to nip Indian unrest in the bud, and to sound a terrible warning. He ordered his soldiers to fire into the defenceless crowd. Three hundred and seventy-nine people were killed and more than 1,200 wounded.

The massacre was a profound shock to Indian people and caused an outcry. It showed that British authority rested, in the end, on ruthlessness, not on any moral force. It was one of the events that sounded the ending of British rule in India. In 1920 Gandhi won the support of Congress in urging that Indians should refuse to co-operate with the British. Government workers, teachers and others disrupted the work of schools and offices for a while. From that time the relationship between Indians and British was never the same. The struggle for Indian freedom began in earnest.

3 On Grandfather's Knee

The Independence movement filled young Indira's life. As a little girl she arranged her dolls in re-enactments of the demonstrations she witnessed on the streets. There were times when her grandfather's house was a focus of the movement, with Congress members always coming and going. Gandhi used to call to have discussions with Motilal and Jawaharlal, and made the acquaintance of little Indira — 'Indu' as she was known to her family.

One of her earliest memories was of going to court at the age of four. She sat on her grandfather's knee as he was sentenced to six months in prison for distributing anti-government pamphlets. Her father was sentenced in another court on the same day.

This was to be part of the pattern of her childhood. Grandfather's house would often be full of activity, and then it would be suddenly quiet. Indira's girlhood was lonely at times, and unsettled. Her schooling was interrupted. Her mother was often ill and her father was frequently absent from home. Either he was travelling widely in the country, making speeches and organizing the Independence movement, or he was serving prison sentences for these very activities.

Anand Bhavan, Indira's childhood home

By the time she was thirteen her father had been
jailed five times. He once remarked wryly that prison
was his 'second home'. He was first jailed in 1921 and
left prison for the last time in 1945. In all, his prison
sentences totalled more than nine years. He missed his
daughter very much and wrote her long letters from
his cells. These were really history lessons and formed
part of her education. The letters were later published
in book form. Nehru also had books sent to Indira.
There was a well-stocked library at Anand Bhavan and
Indira spent hours in it. She was thrilled by the stories
she read of Joan of Arc, the French heroine who had

defied the English in the fifteenth century. Always an imaginative girl, she thought that she herself might become a modern Joan, fighting for her people.

Early photographs show her wearing British school-girl clothes — blouse, skirt and knee socks. Her grandfather and father often dressed like British gentlemen, in suits, waistcoats and ties. But as the Independence movement grew stronger and the family became more deeply involved in it, the Nehrus burnt their western clothing and adopted Indian dress. Indira burnt a favourite doll because it was British. She and her father sometimes wore western clothing in later years; but as an adult she almost always wore the sari, the graceful traditional dress consisting of a single piece of cloth wound around the body.

In 1926 she and her parents sailed to Europe. Her mother was ill with tuberculosis, a lung disease, and doctors recommended that she should go to Switzerland for treatment. Indira attended two schools in Switzerland and learned to speak French well, a skill that she retained all her life. She also learned to ski and to skate, and saw something of European cities. It was on this trip that she first visited Paris and London. Although her mother was ill it was in other ways a happy time because she and her parents were together.

The family returned to India and Indira's father resumed his political work while Indira went to school in Allahabad. Her grandfather, and then her father, were elected president of the Indian National Congress; and both were imprisoned again.

In Allahabad Indira organized a branch of the

Indira with her grandfather, parents and other members of the family

'Monkey Brigade', a junior section of the Congress. The children who joined made flags, addressed envelopes and supplied water to thirsty people at meetings. They also posted notices on walls and carried messages under the noses of the police. This was risky work, but policemen often did not notice the scampering 'monkeys'. For Indira life was hectic. On her thirteenth birthday her father wrote to her from prison and signed his letter: 'Good-bye, little one, and may you grow up into a brave soldier in India's service.'

In 1930 Motilal Nehru was released from prison because his health was deteriorating. He died five months later. Jawaharlal wrote to Indira, 'He would not like us to give in to grief. How can we rest or give in to futile grief when work beckons and the cause of India's freedom demands our service? For that cause he died. For that cause we will live and strive . . . After all, we are his children and have something of his fire and strength and determination in us.'

In 1931 Indira's mother was arrested and imprisoned for a while. Nehru, himself in prison again, wrote to Indira, 'Once a fortnight you may see Mummie and once a fortnight you may see me, and you will carry our messages to each other.' He noted, however, that, 'you must be rather lonely.' He was right.

Indira went to a boarding school in Poona, in western India, and also to a university in Bengal, in the west, which had been founded by Rabindranath Tagore, a great Indian poet. But her happy time here lasted less than a year. Her mother's health was failing and, in 1935, Indira accompanied her to a sanatorium in the Black Forest region of Germany. Her father did not travel with them. He was back in jail for his political activities.

4   Interlude in England

A telegram was delivered to the prison telling Jawaharlal that his wife was very ill. The authorities freed him and he flew to Europe, an adventurous way to travel from India in those days. Kamala was moved to a clinic in Switzerland and it was here, with her husband and daughter beside her, that she died in 1936 at the age of thirty-eight.

Indira stayed in Switzerland for a while to continue her education, and then went to England, to Badminton School, near Bristol. From here she went to Oxford University, in 1937, settling in as an undergraduate at Somerville College to study history, anthropology and administration. In those days there were few women at the university and some crusty old teachers refused to give lectures to them. In common with other women students Indira wore a shapeless cap and short black gown, and walked or bicycled about the town.

Like her primary and secondary schooling, Indira's university education was interrupted. In 1938 she and her father set off on a long and busy tour of Europe. They visited Germany, seeing the signs of impending war. Indira was exhausted by all this travelling — she was still not a strong girl — and she returned to India to spend a winter resting in the northern hills. She badly wanted to devote herself full time to political work, but her father persuaded her to resume her studies in Oxford. She arrived back at her college in the spring of 1939.

The town was dirty, because of the coal fires. And after the warmth of India England seemed particularly damp. The food in most colleges was poor. Indira was not in good health and in 1940 she became ill with pleurisy, a chest infection. She went to a hospital in London and then to Switzerland to recover, returning to Britain by way of Spain. The Second World War was raging and she saw the bombing of London.

Indira with her father in London

She did not complete her university course. Her health was not good, and she desperately wanted to return to India to take a full part in the independence struggle, which was now reaching a peak.

She was relieved to sail for India in 1941. On the ship with her was a handsome young journalist called Feroze Gandhi. Feroze had known the Nehru family since he was a teenager. He had joined the Independence movement and had gone to England, to the London School of Economics, to finish his education. When Indira and her mother were in Germany in 1935 he had visited them there. When Indira went to Oxford he and she became friendly and met often. In time their friendship grew into love. On their return to India, Indira told her father that she wanted to marry Feroze.

Nehru did not like the idea. He thought his daughter should meet more young men before making up her mind about marriage. Other members of the family were shocked — the Indian custom was that marriages should be arranged by parents and it was unusual for young men and women to choose their own partners. Also, Indira and Feroze were of different religions, and marriage between people of different communities was uncommon. Indira was a Hindu and Feroze was a Parsi. Parsis are followers of the Zoroastrian religion, founded in Persia in the sixth century. They believe in a supreme god. Parsis are a very small community and most of them live in the Bombay area.

Indira would not be diverted from her intention to marry Feroze. It was one of the occasions on which she showed that she was strong-willed. Mahatma Gandhi,

24

her friend, supported her. In the end Nehru gave his blessing and Indira and Feroze were married in Allahabad in March, 1942. The couple sat before a sacred fire and then walked around it, repeating their marriage vows.

Indira was now Mrs Gandhi. Neither she nor her husband were related to the Mahatma. Gandhi is an occupation name and means grocer. But it is one of the magical names of India and of history, a name known throughout the world.

In September 1942 the newly married couple were in prison for political activities. Indira was arrested at a rally. Nehru was also back in prison. So was Gandhi. So were many of their supporters. But events in India were moving inexorably to a dramatic conclusion. There was a feeling in the Independence movement that freedom for India was not far off.

5   The Midnight Hour

When she arrived in prison, Indira Gandhi was greeted by her aunt, her father's sister, Mrs Vijaya Lakshmi Pandit. In the years to follow Mrs Pandit was to become a distinguished ambassador for India, and she held the three most important diplomatic jobs, in London, Washington and Moscow.

Indira spent her twenty-fifth birthday in jail. She was released after eight months, because of her poor health, and was reunited with Feroze. Their son, Rajiv, was born in August 1944, and a second boy, Sanjay, was born two years later.

As the Second World War came to an end it became clear to Britain that Indian independence was inevitable. India was aching for its freedom and Britain no longer had the strength, the will, or the wish to remain as ruler. The world was to change rapidly and the British empire was in its final years.

In 1947 Lord Mountbatten, the last British viceroy of India, presided over the final months of British rule and the handing over of power. But, at the same time, the Indian subcontinent was divided and the new country of Pakistan was created.

During the years before independence, some of the

leaders of the millions of Muslims in India campaigned for a separate country to be carved out of India, as a homeland for Muslims. They asserted that Muslims, followers of the Islamic faith who worship one god they call Allah, would be dominated and oppressed by the Hindu majority in independent India.

The creation of Pakistan, an event known as Partition, was a great disappointment to Gandhi, and others in the Congress, who had hoped that India would remain one country when British rule ended. They believed Hindus and Muslims could live together. But feelings between Muslims and Hindus were strong, and the

A map of India showing the borders of East and West Pakistan

Muslim leader, Mohammed Ali Jinnah, was utterly determined that Pakistan should be created.

The new country was in two parts, West Pakistan and East Pakistan, and they were over 1,500 kilometres apart, with all of the broad shoulders of northern India separating them. As soon as the borders were drawn there began one of the great migrations of history as millions of Muslims and Hindus packed their belongings, left their houses and exchanged countries. Five million Muslims journeyed from India to Pakistan. Five million Hindus and Sikhs left Pakistan for India. During the exchange there were terrible massacres, as both sides fell upon each other with sticks and daggers. Trains were attacked and people butchered. This slaughter contributed to a terrible atmosphere of bitterness. About half a million people were killed during the independence period, 1946-48.

Nevertheless the people of India began their existence as an independent democratic country with high hopes. On the eve of independence, with the green, white and saffron flag of India ready to be unfurled in place of the Union Jack, Jawaharlal Nehru, the first prime minister, spoke to the multitudes, 'Long years ago we made a tryst with destiny, and now the time has come when we shall redeem our pledge, not wholly or in full measure, but very substantially. At the stroke of the midnight hour, when the world sleeps, India will awake to life and freedom. A moment comes, which comes but rarely in history, when we step out from the old into the new, when an age ends, when the soul of a nation, long suppressed, finds utterance . . .'

6   Apprentice To Power

As a widower Nehru felt the need to have a companion by his side, someone to confide in and to be a hostess at official receptions and dinners. He chose his daughter. She became his official hostess and helped him entertain many leaders from other countries who visited Delhi. She also travelled with him on his numerous trips abroad. Her upbringing had taught her much about the freedom struggle. Now, at her father's side, she was to gain an education into the workings of a democracy and the realities of power.

She was present at the meetings he had with political leaders in India and overseas. She built up an invaluable store of knowledge, and learnt of the strengths and weaknesses of men who had power. She saw her father speaking in the parliament in Delhi, and discussing and pondering problems at home. The experience was a long apprenticeship under the guidance of an outstanding leader at the height of his powers.

India's early years as an independent country were ones of turmoil. There was strife as millions of people changed sides between India and Pakistan, and there were problems created by streams of refugees. In Delhi

Indira as hostess and companion to her father

Indira braved the anger of Hindu crowds to go to the help of frightened Muslims. Millions of Muslims did not go to Pakistan and chose to remain in India. (Today about a tenth of the people in India are Muslims.)

The strains between India and Pakistan were made worse by a quarrel over the state of Kashmir. Pakistan claimed it at the time of Partition, but it became part of India. In October 1947 the two countries fought a short war over it, sowing the seeds of more bitterness.

Mahatma Gandhi lived only a few months after the Independence he had fought to bring about for so many years. In January 1948, while he was on his way to a prayer meeting in Delhi, he was shot dead by an extremist Hindu. It was a violent end to a life devoted to peace. Hundreds of thousands of people gathered for his funeral procession and cremation by the Jumna river. For Indira it was a deep personal loss. She had often discussed her own problems with him. This saintly man had been her friend and inspiration since she was a little girl. For her, and for India, he had been a guiding light.

With Gandhi gone, the people of India focused all their attention, and their hopes, on Nehru, their undisputed leader. Nehru moved into a large house in Delhi, and his daughter and two grandsons moved in with him. Nehru made heavy demands on Indira and she felt she had a responsibility to help him.

Feroze had a difficult relationship with his father-in-law. He did not like to be known as Nehru's son-in-law and wanted to be regarded as a man in his own right. He plunged into his work, first as a newspaper editor and then as a busy member of parliament. He won a reputation for great honesty and dedication. He had his own house in Delhi. Years later Mrs Gandhi said it was not true that she and Feroze had separated: 'It wasn't an ideally happy marriage. We were very happy at times. We quarrelled tremendously at times. It was partly because both of us were so headstrong, and partly circumstances.'

Feroze Gandhi died in 1960, and his wife was at his bedside. His son, Rajiv, lit the funeral pyre.

Indira accompanied her father on twenty-four foreign tours. She went to the United States, China, Russia, Egypt, Poland and other countries. She and her father attended the Coronation of Queen Elizabeth II in London in 1953.

She also travelled all over India, getting to know the ordinary people and their problems. She worked hard in elections and on Congress party business. The Congress was the strongest political party in the country. In 1959 she became Congress president, a position once held by her father and grandfather. She was then forty-two and she began to demonstrate some of her natural toughness, and the political skills she had learned. She had the makings of a leader.

7   The Seat Of Power

At her father's side, and in her own travels, Indira Gandhi saw clearly how difficult it was to govern an immense country like India and how large its problems were.

India stretches 3,000 kilometres from the Himalayas to the southernmost point of Cape Comorin. It is 2,700 kilometres wide from the edges of China to the Arabian Sea. Its culture is ancient and its people are widely varied in their customs, languages, costume and diet. It is a teeming land of great contrasts. It has much poverty. Millions of people use farming methods that have changed little in thousands of years and live in small villages. On the other hand, it is a modern and developing country with expanding cities, up-to-date industry, fine universities and, in some parts, the most advanced farming methods.

India has fifteen official languages and hundreds of minor ones. Its major language, Hindi, is spoken by about two-fifths of the people. English is spoken by a small minority, a few million people, but it is used throughout the country and is spoken in parliament.

Languages, religion and caste are, from time to time, causes of quarrelling among India's people. But they are also reasons for unity. Most of the language groups are large and cover huge sections of the country. Hinduism is followed by the majority. And the caste system, for all the rivalries between different clans, is an established, stable and well-understood social system.

India was a backward and poor country of 350 million people when it became independent. It had few factories and not much money. Most Indians worked on the land. Farmers were heavily dependent on the monsoon, the wind that brings the annual rains. Every year people waited and watched the weather reports as the monsoon moved northwards. A good monsoon, with heavy rain, was a cause for celebration. A bad monsoon, with only meagre rainfall, meant poor harvests and famine. India had to import food to prevent starvation.

The monsoon is still a natural phenomenon of vital importance to Indian agriculture. But there have been many improvements which have made farmers more productive. The use of fertilizers, pest killers, better irrigation and the introduction of stronger types of corn and rice, have enabled modern India to feed itself.

Nevertheless the demands on food and other resources have grown heavier. The population has more than doubled since independence, partly because of improvements in feeding, public health and disease control. In India today the population is more than 750 million and is increasing at the rate of one million a month.

Mrs Gandhi became familiar with the lot of the

A girl from the Himalayas

Indian people, and their hopes for improvement. She travelled more widely over the country than any other leader before her. She saw for herself the different problems of the desert dwellers of Rajasthan, the mountain people of the Himalayas, the farmers of the great northern plains, the inhabitants of the hot south . . . the dazzling patchwork of India.

In 1962 a long-simmering dispute over borders between India and China boiled over into war. It was a bad time for India. Chinese troops poured over the frontier in the far north-east of India. Mrs Gandhi visited the Indian soldiers at the front. Eventually the Chinese withdrew. But the war was a hard blow for Nehru. He had hoped for unity in Asia. But the last years of his life were clouded by this war between neighbours.

In May 1964 he died in Delhi at the age of seventy-four. India was stunned. The prime minister's life had covered an epoch in the country's history, from the early days of the Independence movement to the development of a modern country. As his country's leader he had built up its industry and education system. He made parliament strong. In India's dealings with foreign countries he set out to keep his country steering a middle course between the big powers of America and Russia. This is called 'non-alignment'. Nehru was an heroic figure in his country's history.

His successor was Lal Bahadur Shastri. He appointed Mrs Gandhi to a place in his government, as Minister for Information and Broadcasting. It was a minor post, but it gave her valuable experience. In 1965 there was another short war between India and Pakistan, which ended indecisively. Mr Shastri died after only two years in office. In January 1966 the Congress party leaders chose Mrs Gandhi to be prime minister, leader of the largest democracy in the world.

'I do not regard myself as a woman,' she said. 'I am a person with a job to do.'

8 Victory . . .

Her first year in power was an uneasy one. The monsoon was bad and the harvest was thin. There was a serious shortage of food. The war with Pakistan in 1965 had been expensive. Hardship led to rioting in several cities. People began to grumble about their new leader and asked what she was doing to help them. It was a bad time for Mrs Gandhi. There was an election in 1967 and the Congress party won by only a narrow margin as the people showed their displeasure with the government.

Within the party itself there was discord, with older men opposing the prime minister. They thought they could control her. But Mrs Gandhi showed her skill and ruthlessness as a political fighter and she was determined to remain leader of India. She split the party and left her opponents out in the cold. She was now more secure and she made it her business throughout her long leadership to surround herself with people she could trust and dominate.

Her fortunes turned. She established herself in firm control of the Congress party and the country and won a handsome victory in the 1971 elections. In that year, too, she enhanced her reputation with her brilliant

With Bengali refugees

handling of the turmoil in East Pakistan.

The people of this region were campaigning for independence. They were governed from West Pakistan, hundreds of kilometres away. They felt too remote from the government. They spoke a different language, Bengali, and had a different culture and traditions. Although they were Muslims too, they felt strongly that they were a different people. But the government in West Pakistan made a determined effort to stamp out the separatist movement. In East Pakistan there was terror as West Pakistan soldiers acted brutally. There was a wave of killing. It was a terrible civil war.

Millions of refugees poured into India from East Pakistan, seeking protection. In all, about nine million people fled. Although they were a big burden they were cared for and fed in India.

Mrs Gandhi said that Pakistan's forces should leave the eastern region. Finally, she sent in her army to drive them out. Fighting lasted twelve days and Pakistan was defeated. Its army surrendered. East Pakistan became the new country of Bangladesh.

The affair was a triumph for Mrs Gandhi. In caring for the refugees she was generous. In fighting the Pakistan army she was decisive. Also, she did not make the mistake of letting the Indian army stay too long in the new country which would have caused resentment. Her standing in India and abroad was high. India was clearly the master of the subcontinent.

9 . . . And Defeat

But the time of glory did not last long. The war, as war always is, was very costly. Again there was a bad monsoon and a poor harvest. The country was tormented by drought. There were food shortages and prices went up in the markets. There was disappointment because too much had been claimed for the 'green revolution' — the improved farming methods. Gradually people became anxious and discontented. There were strikes and demonstrations.

Mrs Gandhi's government became unpopular as the country's woes grew worse. There was high unemployment. India found it could not sell its goods abroad. Oil and petrol prices increased, causing more difficulties.

A political storm grew. Mrs Gandhi's critics blamed her for the troubles. The newspapers attacked her. There were complaints that her close associates were guilty of swindling and bribery. Her government was accused of being dishonest.

Mrs Gandhi felt threatened as the mood of the country became uglier. As the weather grew hotter and more oppressive in June 1975, so the political tension grew. Matters came to a head in Allahabad, the home city of the Nehrus. The high court there gave a ruling that Mrs Gandhi had been guilty of minor offences in her election in 1971 — she had used government staff to help her in her campaign. It was a small matter, but it was against the rules. The penalty was disqualification from holding office. At once her opponents demanded that she leave. They planned a big protest campaign.

But Mrs Gandhi struck first. On the night of 25 June she carried out one of the most controversial acts of her political career. She declared a state of emergency, claiming that there was a threat to the country's security, that India was threatened by disorder. Emotions ran high. She ordered the arrest of her political opponents and they were taken to jail. The press, which had been free, was put under censorship: everything that was published had first to be cleared by a government official. Criticism was kept out of the newspapers. The legal rights of the people were withdrawn. Strikes were banned. Thousands of people were rounded up and imprisoned.

It was as if Mrs Gandhi had turned on a hose of icy water. Everyone was stunned by her sudden and tough action. People complained that Mrs Gandhi had become, overnight, a dictator. She was strongly criticized abroad and was accused of overthrowing India's democracy. She retorted in a speech that, 'sometimes a bitter medicine has to be administered to a patient to cure him'. She claimed that she had acted firmly to save India's democracy.

Some Indians were pleased that Mrs Gandhi had acted so firmly. They thought the country had been running out of control and needed to be put back in

With her sons, Rajiv and Sanjay

order. Businessmen were happy that strikes were
outlawed. People were pleased when Mrs Gandhi
ordered large-scale arrests of smugglers and other
criminals.

She was the absolute power in the land, her authority
unchallenged, her opponents and critics jailed and
silenced. A few people muttered that India had entered
an age of darkness.

During this period, known as the 'emergency', her

43

younger son, Sanjay, became more prominent. Like her father, Mrs Gandhi needed someone close to her, someone she could trust. Her elder son, Rajiv, was not very interested in politics. After his university education in Cambridge he had become an airline pilot and flew with Indian Airlines. He lived a quiet life, out of the public spotlight.

But Sanjay was different. He was fascinated by politics and power. He became leader of the Congress party youth section. He worked at his mother's side and became her right-hand man. He was ambitious and aggressive and had contempt for the normal rules of politics.

Some young people found him exciting and called him the man of the future. Many believed that in time he would succeed his mother as leader of India. And many found that prospect frightening because he seemed so ruthless.

Two things happened in the emergency that were particularly controversial. There was a slum clearance programme in Delhi in which many houses were swept away by bulldozers. The high-handed and brutal nature of this operation made people furious. There was also the government's plan to control population growth. The population was increasing at a very high rate, placing a great strain on the country's food, land, housing, education and health services. Mrs Gandhi's government proposed that people should be medically sterilized to stop them having children. This frightened people, particularly villagers. The stories and rumours of sterilization made the government very unpopular.

44

Meanwhile, there were good monsoon rains and excellent harvests. Prices dropped and people found it easier to get food and other goods. At the beginning of 1977 Mrs Gandhi suddenly announced that there would be elections in March. Her close advisers told her she would win. She herself felt that she would be returned to power. After nineteen months the emergency period was ended, political prisoners were released from jail and the country resumed its democratic ways and voted in the elections.

Mrs Gandhi was wrong in her belief that she would win. The people were angry with her. They were upset by the jailings and the brutalities of the emergency. Election banners said: 'End Dictatorship. Dethrone the Queen.'

Mrs Gandhi and the Congress party were decisively defeated by the Janata party. This was a group of opponents who buried their own differences and united in the single purpose of getting rid of Mrs Gandhi. They detested her. Mrs Gandhi's great rival, Morarji Desai, whom she had jailed in the emergency, was now prime minister in her place. For Indira Gandhi it was the most bitter of times.

10 The Road Back

It was also a tempestuous time. Her opponents sought to make her pay for the emergency. Mrs Gandhi and Sanjay were strongly criticized for what had happened during that period, particularly the arrests and detention of thousands of people. A commission of inquiry was set up and reported to parliament that Mrs Gandhi had been wrong to declare the state of emergency.

In a dramatic scene in the parliament in Delhi she was arrested and taken to jail. Thousands of her supporters demonstrated in the streets and fought with police. An airliner was hijacked in protest at her jailing. After a few days she was released. But plans were made to put her, and Sanjay, on trial.

She was not a person to brood upon defeat, or to be deflected in her aims. She had been knocked down, but she was by no means out. She was convinced that she was the best person to lead India. She had a strong and clear idea of the place of the Nehrus in Indian history. She used all her skill to fight back.

There were a number of things in her favour. She was a Nehru, and that counted for a lot. She had a strong personality and she knew how to talk to ordinary

With people of her country

people. She was the only politician who was known all over the country because she had travelled so widely for many years. Other political leaders were known only in the regions they came from.

Also, the Janata party, her opponent, quickly became unpopular because its members seemed to have very few good ideas. It began to look incompetent. Its members began to quarrel among themselves. The only thing that they agreed upon was their dislike of Mrs Gandhi — and that was not enough.

Mrs Gandhi knew all this. She looked forward to returning to power. She carefully rebuilt her support. She split the Congress party and gathered round her a circle of loyal people, completely devoted to her. The memories of the emergency began to fade in the public mind.

Mrs Gandhi took great care to keep in touch with the people. When there was severe flooding after a storm she flew to the disaster area to comfort the victims. She acted, in fact, as if she were still prime minister. She worked hard and remained prominent in the public eye. As the Janata party crumbled she was seen as firm and resolute. Thus she showed what a good politician she was.

At last the Janata government collapsed. The people were tired of it and it had let them down. Elections were called for January 1980, and Mrs Gandhi threw herself wholeheartedly into the campaign. She criss-crossed the country by road and air, addressing countless meetings. Great crowds waited for hours just to see her, often late into the night. She seemed to be the only person who could offer India real leadership. There was a famous slogan — 'India is Indira, Indira is India.'

She was swept back to power only thirty-three months after losing it. She had been at the bottom, now she was back on top. It was a remarkable performance.

11   The Arrival of Rajiv

Indira Gandhi was now unchallenged leader again. Her picture was everywhere — in the numerous newspapers and news magazines, on wall posters and on giant hoardings beside the main roads of big cities.

There were also many pictures of Sanjay, who was becoming more important. His bespectacled face and his habitual costume of long white shirt and white trousers were familiar to millions of people. His mother relied on him to help her. Some of his friends were included in her new government. He was clearly becoming a force to reckon with.

But India was never to discover how he would use his position at his mother's side. One morning in June 1980 he and a friend went up in a small stunt aircraft from the airfield in Delhi, not far from his home. Sanjay, always headstrong and adventurous, tried a reckless stunt while flying too close to the ground and crashed. He and his passenger were killed instantly.

Sanjay, who was thirty-three, was cremated next day. His mother sat on the ground near the pyre, her sad face lit by the flames, a large crowd pressing around her. The funeral pyre was lit by Rajiv and it was to him that Mrs Gandhi now turned in her shock and grief.

Rajiv was then thirty-six. He had been happy staying in the background, concentrating on his flying career. He was a modest man and avoided trading on his famous surname. When he was flying he used to introduce himself to passengers as 'Captain Rajiv' rather than 'Captain Gandhi'.

He loved his quiet and agreeable life with his wife, Sonia, and their son and daughter. He had met Sonia while they were both studying in England. Sonia was Italian, but she quickly fitted into the new way of life in India. She learnt to speak Hindi and wore saris. She got on well with Mrs Gandhi and sometimes cooked for her. Mrs Gandhi loved Italian food.

Rajiv had a strong sense of duty. Some people complained that Mrs Gandhi was trying to continue a dynasty, a ruling family, by recruiting her son as her lieutenant. But Rajiv said that his mother had to be helped.

He gave up his job with Indian Airlines to be at his mother's side. He and Sonia moved into a house near the prime minister's residence at No. 1, Safdarjang Road, in the heart of Delhi. Rajiv, who was known to dislike politics and some of the ways of politicians, now began to learn the business. He was a purposeful man. Like his father he was known for his straightforwardness and honesty. Indeed he was awarded the nickname of 'Mr Clean'. It was quite a compliment.

Every morning his mother held a darshan in the spacious grounds of her home. This is an Indian tradition. In a darshan a leader meets people informally so that they can express grievances and present

Rajiv and Sonia

petitions. It provides an important opportunity for people to talk to their leaders about their troubles — land problems, oppressive landlords, religious matters, business, taxes and transport. The darshan helps leaders to keep in touch with the mood of the citizens.

After her morning darshan, Mrs Gandhi had a busy programme of meetings and parliamentary business. She travelled abroad — to the United States, Russia and Britain — and presided at international conferences in Delhi. In her dealings with other countries she steered the same course as her father and sought to keep India in the middle, between the giant powers of Russia and America.

She continued her frequent travels within India, addressing huge rallies and visiting people in trouble. She was very proud of the fact that many poor people referred to her as 'Mother'.

She believed that a strong and united India depended on a powerful leader in Delhi. She did not like the idea of regional leaders becoming too important because she feared that they would cause trouble and shake the unity of the whole country. She always tried to have regional leaders who were entirely loyal to her; and some of her big battles were with men who were not in her Congress party and stood up to her and had their own loyal followings.

She found it difficult to trust more than a few people. That is why she recruited her sons to help her. She wanted to feel absolutely secure.

From his unique position close to the top, Rajiv developed a grasp of India's problems and noted how his mother handled them. For example, there was trouble in the state of Assam, in the north-east of the country. The local people did not like the way that immigrants were coming in from Bangladesh and settling down. There were terrible massacres. It was a hard problem to solve because feelings were bitter.

There was also the beginning of trouble in the Punjab, in the north-west of India. It started as a rumble and blew into a threatening storm. Eventually it grew into the crisis that led to Mrs Gandhi's murder.

12   The Gathering Storm

The Punjab is a rich and fertile region and is the homeland of the Sikhs. The Sikh religion was founded in the sixteenth century and Sikhs became a military people, with a reputation as great warriors, in response to the persecution they suffered.

Sikhs have always been excellent soldiers and many of them have made their careers in the army, navy and air force. They are also in the forefront as doctors, engineers, pilots, civil servants, businessmen and farmers. Their skill as farmers made them leaders of the 'green revolution' in which India increased its harvests with improved corn. Because of its good harvests the Punjab is known as 'the bread basket of India'.

There are about 14 million Sikhs. They are only about 2 per cent of the people of India. But their contribution to Indian life is very large. Sikh men are instantly recognizable. They wear turbans and do not shave or cut their hair. They also wear an iron bangle on their wrists. And most of them have the name Singh, meaning lion.

The heart of the Sikh religion is the beautiful Golden Temple in the city of Amritsar. Here the Sikhs' holy

The Golden Temple at Amritsar

book is constantly read aloud and pilgrims come to take a ritual bath in the great pool within the temple walls. Sikhs regard Amritsar as their holy city and the Golden Temple as the holy of holies.

During the late 1970s and early 1980s discontent grew among some of the Sikhs. They felt that they were not given enough recognition for their achievements, and at the same time they became anxious that within Punjab, their own state, they were becoming out-numbered by Hindus. They wanted the government to pay greater respect to their religion and many of them wanted Punjab to have more self-government.

Their own political party split up, so that their leadership was weakened. This was dangerous. Sikh grievances multiplied. Some were big, some were trivial. But even the small ones grew in importance as the atmosphere became worse.

Some Sikhs began to demand that Punjab should become a country independent of India. At the same time a Sikh terrorist movement started and hundreds of people were murdered.

It would have been better, in the early days of the Punjab troubles, to find a way for the Sikhs to run the state government of Punjab. But Mrs Gandhi wanted her own Congress party to run it.

The situation grew steadily more menacing. Terrorists were using the Golden Temple as a refuge and the authorities were reluctant to enter such a holy place to arrest them. Emotions ran high. Mrs Gandhi had failed to nip the grievances in the bud and had allowed matters to fester.

Although the Punjab was plainly a powder keg, she took a fateful decision. In June 1984 she sent in the army to clear the extremists out of the Golden Temple. There was a fierce battle as the extremists resisted with all their might. Hundreds of men, including more than 80 soldiers, were killed. The terrorist leaders lay dead beside their guns.

The attack on the Golden Temple caused a roar of outrage. Even moderate Sikhs who hated the extremists felt upset by the government's assault on their holy place. The Punjab was placed under strict military law and Sikhs felt bruised and angered by the episode.

A few felt that the honour of the whole Sikh people had been hurt. In secret places a number of men vowed they would have their revenge.

13   The Last Day Of October

As usual Mrs Gandhi was awake at 6 a.m., and her servant brought her a pot of tea. She looked at the morning newspapers, bathed and put on an orange-coloured cotton sari. She then went for breakfast with Sonia, her daughter-in-law, and Priyanka and Rahul, her granddaughter and grandson. Rajiv was away in West Bengal. After breakfast the prime minister kissed the children and they set off for school.

Mrs Gandhi's usual morning darshan had been cancelled. Instead she had arranged to give a television interview to the actor and writer Peter Ustinov in the grounds of her home. He and the camera crew were already waiting for her on a lawn surrounded by rose bushes.

As she walked rapidly along the garden path to keep the appointment, two Sikh bodyguards, men she trusted, opened fire, one with a pistol, the other with a sub-machine gun. Mrs Gandhi fell to the ground. It was about 9.15 on 31 October 1984. The assassins were seized. Hearing the shots, Sonia rushed from the house.

Mrs Gandhi was carried to a car and, with Sonia cradling her, was driven to hospital. She was hurried to

With her grandson

an operating theatre and doctors fought for hours, trying to save her. But life had gone.

In West Bengal Rajiv was given the news and boarded an aircraft for Delhi. Outside the hospital where Mrs Gandhi lay, thousands of people gathered.

At last the news of her death was broadcast over All India Radio and on television. Shortly after his return to Delhi Rajiv Gandhi took the oath of office as prime minister. He made a broadcast appealing for calm, but there was violence in Delhi and other parts of the country as enraged mobs turned on Sikh families in revenge. Hundreds of Sikhs were killed, thousands of their homes and shops were burnt. Many Sikhs fled and hid, and many found protection in the homes of Hindus. It was an ugly episode in India's history.

In Indira Gandhi India had a remarkable and dedicated leader, a woman utterly devoted to her country. She was determined that India should be united, strong and progressive. As we have seen, her methods were often controversial. The task of leading India is always formidable and Mrs Gandhi responded to the challenges with great courage and style. Her energy in the service of her country was phenomenal. She built up a firm relationship with her people that was at the heart of her popularity and power. She was, at home and abroad, the living symbol of India, the best-known Indian personality. She provided India with a sense of continuity and purpose and pride.

Important Events in the
Life of Indira Gandhi (1917-1984)

1917   Born in Allahabad, Uttar Pradesh State.
1938   Joins the Congress party.
1942   Marries Feroze Gandhi. Goes to prison for political activity.
1947   Becomes confidante and official hostess to her father as he leads independent India.
1959   Elected president of the Congress party.
1966   Begins the first of four terms as prime minister.
1971   Directs and wins war against Pakistan as Bangladesh is born.
1975   Declares an emergency and jails her opponents as civil unrest spreads.
1977   Defeated in elections.
1980   Returns to power.
1984   June: Sends troops into the Golden Temple in Amritsar. October: Assassinated at her home in Delhi.

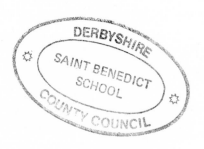